To BMG.F family

What a wonderful night with you
Sharing Tata's Legacy.

we look forward to welcome
you back Home.

[signature]

Made With Love

09/04/24

A PLACE OF REFLECTION
SANCTUARY MANDELA

NELSON MANDELA
FOUNDATION
Living the legacy

For my children
Mkhululi, Sinethemba,
Mnqophiso and Lubambo

Xoliswa Ndoyiya
Made With Love

Recipes and Memories from
Nelson Mandela's Personal Chef

———

Photography Cameron Gibb

Blackwell&Ruth.

"There is one respect
in which I dwarf all my
contemporaries or at
least about which I can
confidently claim to
be second to none — a
healthy appetite. There
was a time when I could
polish off enormous
quantities of food in any
order. I could start from
pudding backwards & feel
just as happy & contented
at the end of it all."

— Nelson Mandela

Contents

Foreword

Sis' Xoli, as she is affectionately called by many members of our family, started working for Tat'omkhulu (grandfather) in 1992, until Tat'omkhulu's passing in December 2013. It was 21 years of excellent service. She served Tat'omkhulu with her heart and soul, with love and care, and with great distinction. I always knew that when Sis' Xoli was around, Tat'omkhulu was in great hands. Her love and commitment to Tat'omkhulu and our family was truly remarkable, heartwarming and extra special.

There is nothing more comforting than coming home to a delicious home-cooked meal and your taste buds responding in tingling anticipation. The aroma of herbs and spices from the kitchen would draw me in and give me a sense of comfort as soon as I walked through the door, leaving my troubles of the day outside.

To many of us in the family, Sis' Xoli was more than Tat'omkhulu's personal chef, she was a big sister and a mother to many of my younger cousins and our children. The only dampener to her incredible labour of love and care was the fact that her own family and children did not benefit as much as Tat'omkhulu and his family did.

In the kitchen she cooked up a storm, and many family members developed a preference for her special dishes. For me, each meal tasted like food prepared at an à la carte five-star restaurant — breakfast, lunch, and supper equally delectable. E-V-E-R-Y D-A-Y!! She generously shared her recipes with us, and at the end she would write 'sprinkled with love'. Very true indeed, I tasted the love in each meal she prepared.

I am forever grateful to Sis' Xoli for the precious gift of love and memories she helped me create during our special meals together as a family — at home in Houghton, and in Qunu in the Eastern Cape.

Qunu was extra special for many reasons: It is in the countryside and far from the madding crowd; it is where Tat'omkhulu grew up, and as we enjoyed many of our precious meals he would reminisce about his childhood memories as a young boy, running and playing on the rolling and beautiful hills of Qunu; being under one roof helped Tat'omkhulu bond with his family after being deprived of a normal family life for 27 years while he languished in prison; the simple joy of what many families take for granted — being together as a family under one roof, sharing stories and laughing together over delicious meals was truly priceless. I could see that Tat'omkhulu was at peace and enjoyed watching each one of us talking excitedly. He had clearly missed this, and savoured each moment; and as a family we got to know each other a little bit better while enjoying each carefully prepared meal — a lifelong gift.

Sis' Xoli, I say a very big and hearty thank you over, and over again. The gift you have bequeathed us is timeless and priceless. Your role in making my precious memories is indelible and can never be diminished. You are truly precious to me, and you will remain precious forever and ever.

Enkosi kakhulu Sis' Xoli (thank you very much Sis' Xoli).

With love and appreciation,
Nandi Mandela
Nelson Mandela's granddaughter

Introduction

My love of food began early on, as a young woman growing up in South Africa's Eastern Cape. As the eldest daughter, it was my responsibility to prepare meals while my mother worked. I learned the basics of cooking and became curious about experimenting with food and creating recipes of my own. My grandmother would also bring us delicious home-cooked meals, and I think these experiences helped me discover the powerful connection between food, love and comfort.

I was working as a chef at an aged-care facility after I had moved to Johannesburg in my twenties, when my life changed overnight. It was 1992 and a friend of mine arranged for a job interview for me to "cook for an icon". I wasn't looking for a job at the time, but I passed the interview and was offered the role. So I said yes, and was taken to meet Tata Madiba (Tata is the isiXhosa word for 'father', Madiba is Nelson Mandela's clan name). He smiled, invited me to sit, and then asked me what my clan name was. "Mamqadai", I said. He said: "I believe you are a great cook, but do you think you can cook our own [isiXhosa] food?" Without hesitation, I said "Yes, Tata." I had the job.

At first it was only me and one other staff member that lived in the house with Tata — the other household staff would come and go during the day. Our days began early, with Tata taking his first cup of coffee at 3.30 a.m. I would bring it to his door, where he would greet me warmly, then have me follow him out to the garden for his morning exercise. Breakfast was prepared by 6.30 a.m., and was the same every day — fresh fruit, porridge with nuts and raisins and sometimes bacon, eggs, green salad and a slice of home-baked bread toast with marmalade. I quickly learned that Tata liked consistency and punctuality! And yet one morning, after eighteen years, he decided he would have Frosties with his grandchildren instead of porridge. Tata never ate sugar, chocolates or sweets, until that day. The next morning, he wanted Frosties again. When I asked him why, he told me he had only eaten porridge all those years to honour his mother, who made it for him when he was growing up. Now he felt ready to eat whatever he wanted, and at that moment it meant sharing a common food with his grandchildren. The same thing happened when Tata saw his grandchildren and Mama Graça [Machel] enjoying double-toffee ice cream. He asked for a taste only, and then there he was asking for double-toffee ice cream for dessert again and again. For him, family and food went hand-in-hand.

For twenty-two years I had the privilege of being Tata's personal chef, and I cooked many meals for Tata, his colleagues, his friends and his family. His grandchildren stayed often, and my live-in colleague and I spent so much time looking after them that they took to calling us "Mama". Tata also had a habit of inviting other children to the house, feeding them and asking them about their schoolwork — he would read about them in the paper or somehow hear about them, and next thing there they were, sitting at the table. He simply loved children and wanted to look after them all.

It was Tata's nature to be warm and hospitable to all, and by default my mission was to welcome people visiting the house with comforting, home-cooked dishes. And Tata, in his generous nature, never failed to acknowledge my efforts. One evening when I was serving food to a group of visiting dignitaries, he called me over to the table and said: "Xoli, you know me, I don't take credit for anybody. These people keep saying thank you to me. I didn't go to the kitchen to cook for them, so they must say thank you to you." That was Tata's way of telling us, "When you respect people, they will respect you back". And that was the Tata I grew to know: always generous, always compassionate and always perceptive. Tata used to look me straight in the eye and say: "Xoli, when I ask people to come to the house, please do exactly what you do every day, don't stop doing it. You fill up my table with a smile and you're giving us food made with love."

So *Made With Love* isn't just another cookbook; it is a thank you to Tata, a way of passing the baton so that we can all share the things he valued most, with the ones we love. Because at his table you wouldn't see just one person — a Black person, a white person — you'd see all people coming together, sharing together and giving to others through food made with love.

— Xoliswa Ndoyiya

"Tata once said: 'My mother was not that great
a cook, but when she cooks for us, we feel
comfortable because it is food from home.
It's just how we like it.'"

— Xoliswa Ndoyiya

"... I long for amasi —
the food for which
I loved to sharpen my
teeth and to stretch out
my tummy, the one that
I really enjoyed, that
went straight into my
blood and into my heart
and produced perfect
contentment."

– Nelson Mandela

TATA M
BREAI

ADIBA'S
ΚFAST

Fruit Platter

Ingredients
....

pineapple

melon

orange

passionfruit

blueberries

grapes

Method
....

Wash all fruit. Remove hard skin from pineapple and cut into quarters before slicing. Remove skin from melon and slice. Leave skin on oranges and halve and then slice. Halve passionfruit.

....

Cook's note: Fresh fruit is always best — most nutritious and delicious — when in season, so you should adapt this list according to whatever is in season where you are. This is an example of the fruit I would prepare for Tata Madiba.

"Tata Madiba started every day with fresh fruit, followed by porridge mixed with nuts, raisins and sultanas. And coffee, always coffee. I served that to him every day for 18 years."

Umphokoqo
Porridge

Serves	Ingredients	Method
6–10	2 cups water 1 tsp salt 3 cups maize meal dried fruit and nuts, to garnish	Put the water and salt in a medium-sized lidded saucepan over medium-high heat and bring to the boil. Add the maize meal, cover, and bring back to the boil. Once the maize meal is boiling, stir it with a fork until the water is absorbed and the maize meal is crumbly and not sticking together. Cover again, reduce the heat, and cook until it is soft and fluffy, about 25 minutes. Sprinkle with dried fruit and nuts, and serve. Tata always liked his umphokoqo served with warm milk, but you can serve it with cold milk or amasi (umphokoqo namasi, or porridge with amasi, see recipe page 42).

Cook's note: Maize meal, or cornmeal, is also known as mielie-meal, 'mielie' being the Afrikaans word for a corn cob or maize plant. It can be cooked to a crumbly consistency to make umphokoqo, or to a smoother consistency to make uphuthu or pap.

"Tata loved this dish so much I once had to
arrange for it to be smuggled into England.
Tata was visiting London and I got a call
to say that Tata was not himself — he
was missing his umphokoqo. So I cooked
some up and we wrapped it up nicely and
wrote on the outside 'The President's
Medication', which is how it was able
to be smuggled into Tata's hotel."

DRI

NKS

Amasi
Sour Milk

Makes	Ingredients	Method

1 litre

1 litre fresh cow's milk
(unpasteurised and refrigerated)

....

Cook's note: Also known as 'maas', amasi is soured or fermented milk commonly used as a drink or as an accompaniment to umphokoqo (see recipe page 36). It is traditionally made in a calabash, a dried hollowed-out gourd that is commonly used in the preparation of African cuisine, but you can use a glass jar with a lid or stopper.

Pour the milk into a calabash or jar and seal with the stopper or lid, not too tight – the fermentation process will release gas, which could cause the vessel to burst if pressure builds up inside it.

Leave the milk to sit at room temperature until it has separated into curds (ingqaka) and whey (intloya). In warm weather this will take 3–4 days, and in colder weather up to 10 days.

Remove the stopper and pour out and discard the whey (or keep to use separately), then serve.

It will keep for up to 14 days in the fridge.

Ginger Drink

Makes	Ingredients	Method
Approximately 20 litres	20 litres lukewarm water	Mix all the ingredients together in a large vessel and leave to stand overnight. Make sure the vessel is large enough to allow for an increase in volume as foam will form on top.
	50 g ground ginger	
	2.5 kg brown sugar	
	20 g (2 packets) tartaric acid (cream of tartar)	
	10 g (1 sachet) instant dry yeast	Strain the liquid and pour into bottles.
	pineapple and blueberries or other fresh fruit to garnish (optional)	Serve cold, garnished with fruit such as pineapple and blueberries if desired.
		It will keep stoppered for up to 14 days in the fridge, but once opened it will lose its effervescence.

"Tata said that when he drank this, it reminded him of his mother, Nosekeni Fanny, who would make it at Christmas time. She would bake bread mixed with sultanas, raisins and dates so they could pretend they were eating Christmas cake, and serve it with ginger beer."

"The prison authorities liked to say that we received a balanced diet; it was indeed balanced — between the unpalatable and the inedible."

— Nelson Mandela

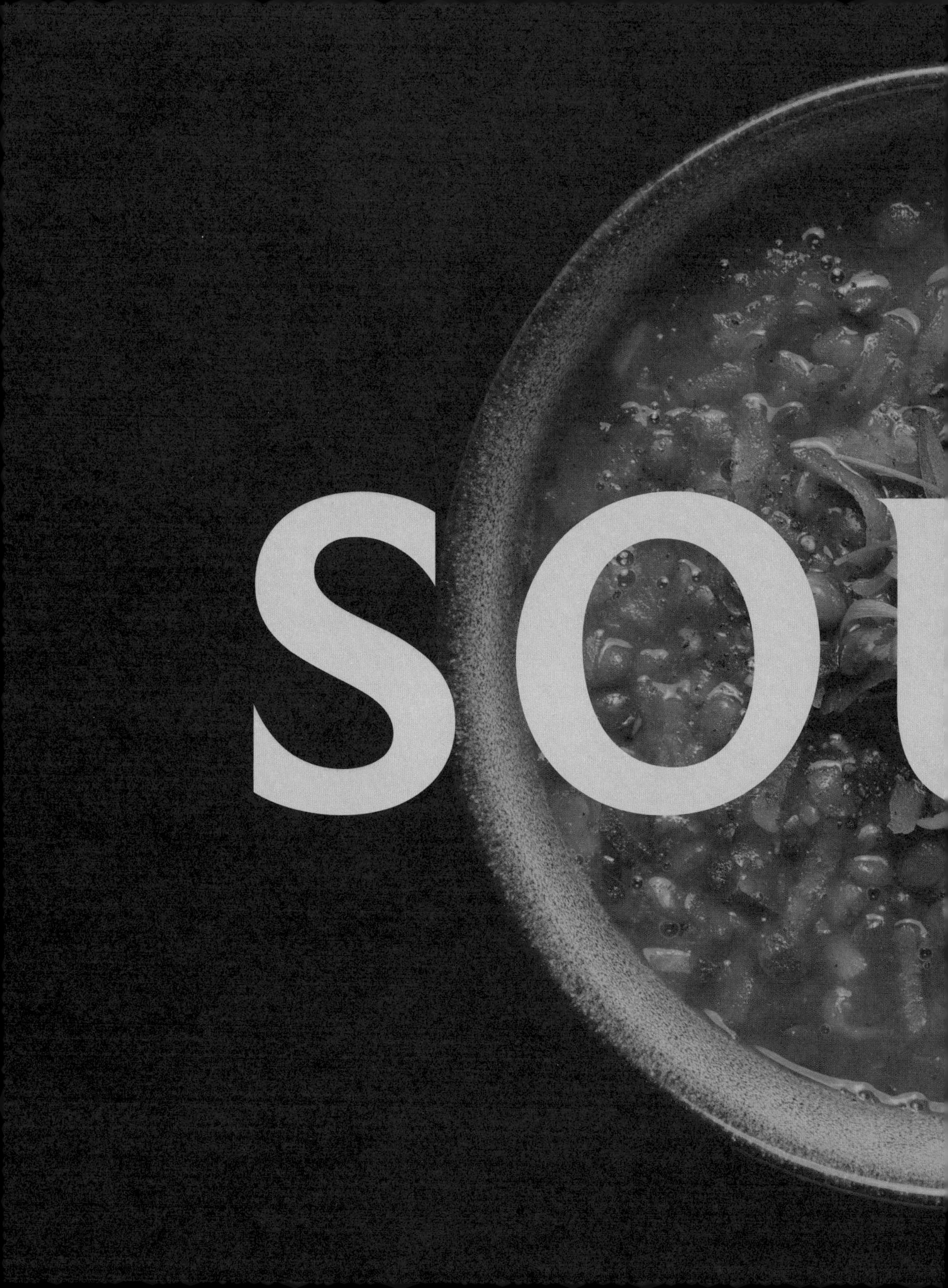
SOU

UPS

Lentil Soup

Serves	Ingredients	Method
4–6	2 cups brown or green lentils	Put the lentils in a medium-sized bowl and cover with water. Leave to soak for 1 hour.

Ingredients

2 cups brown or green lentils
100 ml olive oil
1 medium-sized onion, finely chopped
2 garlic cloves, finely chopped
1 medium-sized potato, peeled and grated
2 large carrots, peeled and grated
1 litre water
2 chicken stock cubes
salt and freshly ground black pepper
microgreens to garnish (optional)

Method

Put the lentils in a medium-sized bowl and cover with water. Leave to soak for 1 hour.

Drain and rinse the lentils. Transfer to a medium-sized saucepan and cover with water. Cook them over medium heat until soft, about 15 minutes.

Heat the oil in a large pot over low heat and fry the onion and garlic until the onion is soft and brown.

Add the lentils, potato, carrot, water and stock cubes and cook until the vegetables are soft, about 15 minutes. If the soup is too thick for your liking, thin out with some extra water or stock.

Season with salt and freshly ground black pepper and serve, garnished with microgreens if desired.

Mushroom Chowder

Serves	Ingredients	
6–8	**Chowder**	**Mushrooms**
	2 tsp vegetable oil	1 tbsp vegetable oil
	2 cloves garlic	1 large onion, chopped
	2 sprigs fresh thyme, leaves finely chopped	2 garlic cloves, crushed
	1 stalk of lemongrass	1 kg button mushrooms, chopped
	1 cup white wine	paprika, to garnish (optional)
	40 g cake flour	chopped chives, to garnish (optional)
	500 ml fish stock	
	500 ml fresh cream	

Method

To make the chowder, heat oil in a medium-sized saucepan over a medium-high heat and sauté garlic until soft, taking care it doesn't burn. Add thyme, lemongrass and wine, mix well and stir until it boils. Mix flour and stock to a paste and add to the chowder mixture. Simmer for 5–10 minutes until the mixture is thick and creamy, stirring continuously. Remove from heat and set aside.

In another saucepan, heat the second measure of oil and fry onion and garlic until golden brown. Add the mushrooms, season with salt and pepper and cook until they start to soften.

Return chowder to the stove, add the cooked mushroom mixture and cook for a further 5 minutes. Add fresh cream and stir to combine. If the soup is too thick, add more water a little at a time to achieve desired consistency.

Serve hot, sprinkled with paprika and scattered with chives, if desired.

....

Cook's note: Cake flour is a finely milled flour with a lower protein content than all-purpose flour, and is often referred to as 'extra-fine' or 'super-fine' flour. If you can't find 'cake' or 'fine' flour, you can substitute it with all-purpose flour mixed with cornflour — for every cup of flour required, remove 2 tablespoons of the flour and replace with 2 tablespoons of cornflour.

Creamy Butternut Soup

Serves	Ingredients	Method
6–8	1 kg butternut squash, peeled, deseeded and roughly chopped	Preheat the oven to 180°C.

Ingredients

1 kg butternut squash, peeled, deseeded and roughly chopped

2 tbsp vegetable oil

500 ml fresh cream, plus additional to serve

1 medium-sized onion, finely chopped

2 litres hot water

3 vegetable stock cubes

1 tbsp chopped fresh basil leaves

ground nutmeg, to garnish (optional)

microgreens, to garnish (optional)

Method

Preheat the oven to 180°C.

Rub the butternut with oil. Place in an ovenproof dish, season with salt and pepper and pour over the cream.

Roast for 20 minutes until soft and golden brown.

Transfer butternut to a large saucepan. Add onion, water and stock cubes, bring to boil and cook for 15 minutes. Add fresh basil and cook for another 5–10 minutes.

Transfer carefully to a blender or food processor and blend until completely smooth.

Serve, garnished with a drizzle of cream, a sprinkle of ground nutmeg and a scattering of microgreens, if desired.

Cook's note: Butternut squash, known in Australia and New Zealand as butternut pumpkin, has a sweet, nutty taste and makes a delicious, rich soup.

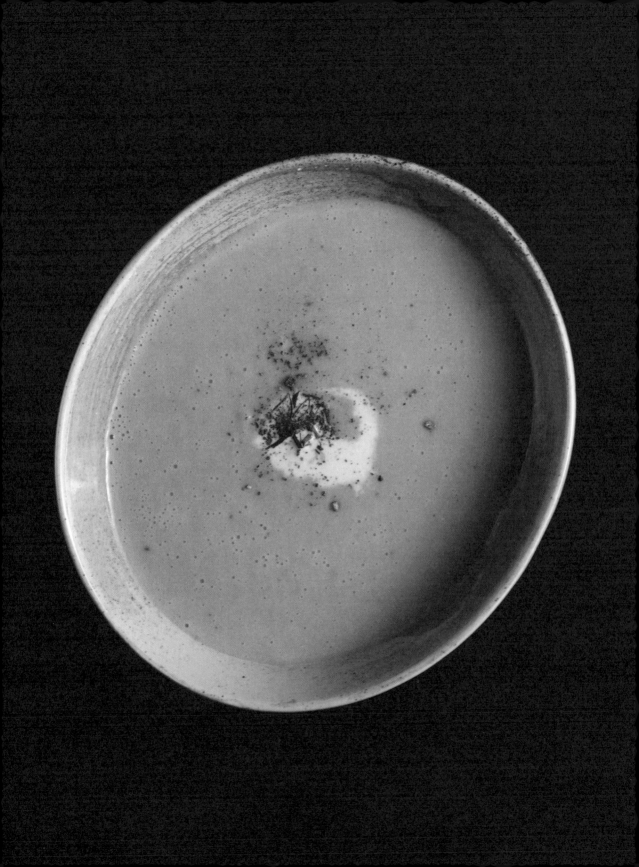

Bean Soup

Serves	Ingredients	Method

6–8

800 g dry sugar (pinto) beans
800 g dry red kidney beans
800 g dry butter (lima) beans
3–4 vegetable stock cubes, dissolved in
   2 cups of boiling water
3 tbsp vegetable oil
2 medium-sized onions, chopped
3 garlic cloves, chopped
1 tbsp finely grated ginger
500 g dry green lentils
6 large tomatoes
microgreens, to garnish (optional)

Combine beans in a large saucepan. Rinse and drain, then add the vegetable stock. Add water if needed to cover the beans. Cover with a lid and bring to the boil, then reduce heat and cook covered for 1 hour, until soft.

In a pan heat the oil and sauté onions, garlic and ginger until soft. Add to the beans with the lentils and cook for a further 30–45 minutes.

Bring a small pot of water to the boil, add the tomatoes and cook until skin is burst, about 20 to 30 seconds. Once cool, chop tomatoes. Blend until completely smooth, then add to the beans and lentils and stir and mix well.

Season with salt and cracked pepper and scatter with microgreens if desired, and serve.

"Tata loved this because he ate a lot of beans growing up. Beans and rice is a popular local dish but Tata didn't like rice and always just wanted the beans, so I created this bean soup for him."

Leek & Potato Soup

Serves	Ingredients	Method
6–8	75 ml vegetable oil	In a large saucepan over medium heat, heat the oil and sauté the onion and garlic until soft and glossy.
	1 large onion, chopped	
	2 garlic cloves, chopped	Add potato, leek, celery, hot water and stock and bring to the boil. Reduce the heat and cook until the potatoes are soft, about 20 minutes.
	4 large potatoes, peeled and chopped	
	8 large leeks, white parts chopped	
	4 celery stalks, chopped	
	2 litres hot water	
	3 vegetable stock cubes	Add the cream and blend the soup until completely smooth.
	500 ml fresh cream	
	microgreens, to garnish (optional)	Season with salt and cracked pepper and scatter with microgreens if desired, and serve.

SAL
& STA

ADS

RTERS

Asparagus & Melon with Avocado

Serves

3–4

Ingredients

500 g asparagus, washed and any
  tough ends removed

120 g baby spinach leaves

1 medium-sized ripe avocado, halved
  then sliced thinly lengthwise

½ melon of choice, cut into 2cm chunks
  or scooped into balls

3 radishes, thinly sliced

citrus dressing (see recipe page 146)

3 tbsp crumbled feta

microgreens, to garnish (optional)

1 tsp black pepper

½ tsp salt

Method

Blanche the asparagus by plunging it
into boiling water for 3–4 minutes, then
cooling in cold water for 2 minutes.

Arrange the spinach on a serving platter
or plate, then decoratively arrange
the asparagus, avocado, melon and
radish. Drizzle the citrus dressing over
salad. Top with the crumbled feta and
microgreens, if using, season with salt
and pepper, and serve.

"Tata loved fruit and he also loved vegetables
so one day I decided to experiment to see if he
would like the two combined together in one
dish. Happily it passed the test and became a
regular on the menu."

Umngqusho
Samp & Beans

Serves	Ingredients	Method

6–8

500 g samp, well rinsed

800 g dried sugar (pinto) beans, well rinsed

1 small onion, chopped

½ cup chopped leek

2 beef stock cubes, dissolved in
1 cup of boiling water

3 tbsp butter

Cook's note: Samp is dried, coarsely broken corn known in Afrikaans as 'stampmielies'. It is often cooked in combination with beans to make umngqusho, a popular local staple dish that was one of Tata's favourites. If you can't find samp, you can substitute it with any dried beans, dried chickpeas or polenta.

Place the samp and beans together in a medium-sized lidded saucepan. Cover with water, then cover with the lid and place over medium-high heat. Bring to the boil then reduce the heat and cook for 1 hour. Do not stir while cooking or it will become excessively starchy, but keep checking to see that the mixture is not sticking to the bottom of the saucepan, adding more water if necessary.

Add the onion, leek and stock and cook for a further 1 hour, until the beans and samp and vegetables are soft. Season with salt and pepper, add the butter and stir with a wooden spoon to mix. If it looks dry, add a touch more water.

Serve with umleqwa (see recipe page 98), umsila (see recipe page 110), or your favourite main dish.

Roasted Aubergine Salad

Serves	Ingredients	Method
6—8	500 g aubergine (eggplant)	Preheat oven to 150°C.

Serves

6—8

Ingredients

500 g aubergine (eggplant)
400 g baby marrow (zucchini)
500 g red peppers (capsicum)
600 g cherry tomatoes
coriander and lime dressing
  (see recipe page 146)
Parmesan, shaved, to serve
rocket leaves, to serve

....

Image on following page

Method

Preheat oven to 150°C.

Thinly slice the aubergine using a mandolin. Lay on a baking tray, season, and roast for 3—5 minutes. Remove the tray from the oven, then remove the aubergine from the tray and set aside.

Slice the baby marrow into ribbons and roast for 2—3 minutes. Remove the tray from the oven, then remove the marrow from the tray and set aside.

Halve the red peppers and roast for 10 minutes. Remove from the oven, leave until cool enough to handle, remove the skin, and cut into thin strips.

Halve the cherry tomatoes and combine with the aubergine, pepper and baby marrow in a bowl. Dress with coriander and lime dressing, top with Parmesan and rocket leaves and serve.

Shrimp & Lentil Salad

Serves	Ingredients	Method

4–6

Ingredients

1 cup brown or green lentils, rinsed

5 cups water

2 cups frozen shelled and deveined medium-sized shrimp

2 tbsp lemon juice

boiling water

1 small onion, thinly sliced

1 green apple, cored and cut into chunks (not peeled)

1 stalk celery, thinly sliced

cider vinaigrette (see recipe page 147)

Method

Combine the lentils, water and a pinch of salt in a medium-sized saucepan and bring to the boil over high heat. Reduce heat to a low simmer, cover and cook for 10–15 minutes, or until the lentils are tender but still hold their shape. Drain well.

Put the shrimp and lemon juice in a small dish with enough boiling water to cover and leave for 3–5 minutes, or until shrimp turns pink. Drain well and combine with the lentils in a serving dish. Add apple and celery.

Spoon the cider vinaigrette over the shrimp and lentils, mix well and serve.

Mushroom & Samp Risotto

Serves	Ingredients	
6–8	2 cups samp (see note page 64)	1 tbsp chopped fresh thyme leaves
	75 ml olive oil	1 cup mushroom stock
	1 large onion, chopped	2 tbsp crumbled feta
	1 tbsp crushed garlic	1 cup grated Parmesan
	1 kg enoki mushrooms, chopped	

Method

Put the samp into a large bowl and rinse and drain it. Transfer to a large heavy-based saucepan and add enough water to cover. Cook on a high heat for 40 minutes, checking the water level as it cooks to make sure the samp remains covered. Lower the heat and continue cooking, continually checking the water level, until the samp is soft but still slightly firm to the bite. Remove from the heat, rinse the starch away, and drain. Set aside.

Heat the oil in a large saucepan over medium-high heat and fry onion and garlic until soft, taking care not to burn. Add the mushrooms, thyme and salt and pepper. Mix well and simmer until mushrooms are soft and cooked through.

Put the mushroom stock into a separate saucepan over medium-high heat and bring to the boil. Add the cooked samp, return to the boil, and let it boil for 5 minutes. Add the cooked mushroom mixture and keep stirring until well combined. Add the feta and cook, stirring for 3 minutes, until creamy.

Add the Parmesan and stir, mixing well. Season with salt and pepper and serve.

"This is a modern interpretation of umngqusho (see recipe page 64) that was created by one of the chefs at Sanctuary Mandela and is served in the hotel restaurant."

"I was no more than five when I became a herd boy looking after sheep and calves in the fields . . . It was in the fields that I learnt how to knock birds out of the sky with a slingshot, to gather wild honey and fruits and edible roots, to drink warm, sweet milk straight from the udder of a cow, and to catch fish with twine and sharpened pieces of wire."

— Nelson Mandela

FISH
SEAF

H &
OOD

Creamy Fish on Roasted Vegetables

Serves	Ingredients	Method

4–6

Ingredients

1 cup sugar snaps or broccoli florets

½ cup roughly chopped carrots

1 cup seeded and cubed butternut squash (see note page 54)

1 cup sliced sweet potato

1 cup sliced baby marrow (zucchini)

½ red pepper (capsicum), seeds removed and cut lengthwise

½ cup olive oil

creamy cheese sauce (see recipe page 148)

600 g yellowtail

2 tbsp freshly squeezed lemon juice

microgreens, to garnish (optional)

....

Cook's note: The yellowtail, also referred to as the yellowtail amberjack, is a medium-sized fish that is found throughout the Pacific and Atlantic oceans, mainly in the Southern Hemisphere. If you can't source yellowtail, then arctic char, bluefish, mackerel, mahi mahi, ocean trout, striped bass, tilefish and wahoo are good substitutes.

Method

Preheat the oven to 160°C.

Put the sugar snaps or broccoli, carrot, butternut, sweet potato, baby marrow and pepper into an ovenproof dish or pan, season with salt and pepper, and pour over 2 tablespoons of the olive oil, mixing well to coat.

Roast for 25–30 minutes, or just until the vegetables still retain their crunch. Switch off the oven and keep vegetables warm inside.

While the vegetables are cooking, make the creamy cheese sauce.

Heat the remaining olive oil in a frying pan over medium-high heat. Season fish with salt and pepper. Fry fish for 5 minutes, then turn and fry for a further 5 minutes. Pour lemon juice over the fish then set aside.

Arrange the vegetables on a serving platter, place fish decoratively on top, pour creamy cheese sauce over the fish, garnish with microgreens, if using, and serve.

Hot Prawn Curry

Serves	Ingredients	Method

6–8

5 medium-sized tomatoes

¼ cup olive oil

2 medium-sized onions, finely chopped

1 tbsp crushed garlic

1 tbsp hot curry powder

1 tbsp masala curry powder

1 tbsp paprika

1 tbsp dried chilli flakes

2 kg prawns, peeled, deveined and cleaned

1 cup water

¼ cup fresh chopped coriander leaves, plus extra to serve

basmati rice with toasted coconut and tomato and red onion salsa in poppadom baskets (see recipe page 144) (optional)

"Tata loved genuine Indian cuisine so much that one day he took me to the Indian Consulate so their chef could show me how to make this hot prawn curry, just like they do in India."

Bring a small pot of water to the boil, add the tomatoes and cook until skin is burst, about 20 to 30 seconds. Once cool, deseed and grate tomatoes.

Heat the oil in a large frying pan over medium-high heat and fry the onions until soft and golden, about 5 minutes.

Add the garlic, curry powder, masala curry powder, paprika and chilli flakes and stir. Cook for a few minutes until fragrant. Add the tomatoes and cook over a low heat until a thick sauce forms, about 5 minutes.

Add the prawns and water and bring to the boil then reduce the heat to low, cover with a lid and simmer for about 20 minutes. Season and stir in half the coriander.

Garnish with extra coriander and serve with basmati rice with toasted coconut and tomato and red onion salsa in poppadom baskets, if desired.

Spicy Butterfly Fried Prawns

Serves

4—6

Ingredients

Marinade

175 ml olive oil

75 ml fresh lemon juice

1 tbsp paprika

2 tbsp crushed garlic

2 tbsp chilli flakes

2 kg prawns, deveined and cleaned

green salad, to serve

....

Image on previous page

Method

To make the marinade combine the olive oil, lemon juice, paprika, garlic and chilli flakes in a large bowl, mixing well.

Cut the prawns in half lengthways, leaving the middle intact so they open up like a butterfly. Season with salt and pepper, then place them into the marinade, turning to coat. Leave to marinate for 10 minutes.

Remove the prawns from marinade and put the excess marinade aside.

Heat the oil in a frying pan over medium-high heat and fry the prawns, pressing to keep the butterfly shape, until the shell is pinkish in colour and the flesh is golden brown on the meaty side, about 4—5 minutes. Arrange on a serving platter.

Pour the reserved marinade into the pan and let it simmer until a nice thick sauce is formed. Pour on top of the prawns.

Serve with a green salad.

Baked Whole Fish

Serves

6–8

Ingredients

Marinade

¼ cup freshly squeezed lemon juice

1 tbsp crushed garlic

2 tbsp fish spice, or substitute with
  1 tbsp salt and ½ tbsp pepper

1 tbsp dried thyme

¼ cup olive oil

3 tbsp peri-peri powder or dried
  chilli flakes

1 medium-sized (approx.1.5 kg)
  firm-fleshed fish

1 medium-sized tomato, thinly sliced

1 medium-sized onion, thinly sliced

3 lemon slices, to garnish

steamed broccoli or other vegetable
  of choice, to serve (optional)

....

Cook's note: Peri-peri — or piri-piri — chillies
are also known as African bird's eye chillies.
Peri-peri powder can be easily substituted
with dried chilli flakes, or if using fresh,
habanero or Scotch bonnet chilli peppers.

Image on following page

Method

Mix all marinade ingredients together in
a large dish or container big enough for
the fish.

Make three shallow cuts on each
side of the fish and immerse in the
marinade, making sure it is well coated
on both sides. Set aside to marinate for
15 minutes.

Preheat the oven to 180°C.

Remove the fish from the marinade and
place in an ovenproof dish. Place onion
and tomato slices on top of the fish.
Cover with foil and bake for 45 minutes.
Remove foil and cook for a further
5 minutes, or if you like your fish crispy,
remove foil earlier.

Garnish with lemon slices, and serve
with steamed broccoli or your favourite
vegetable side.

CHIC

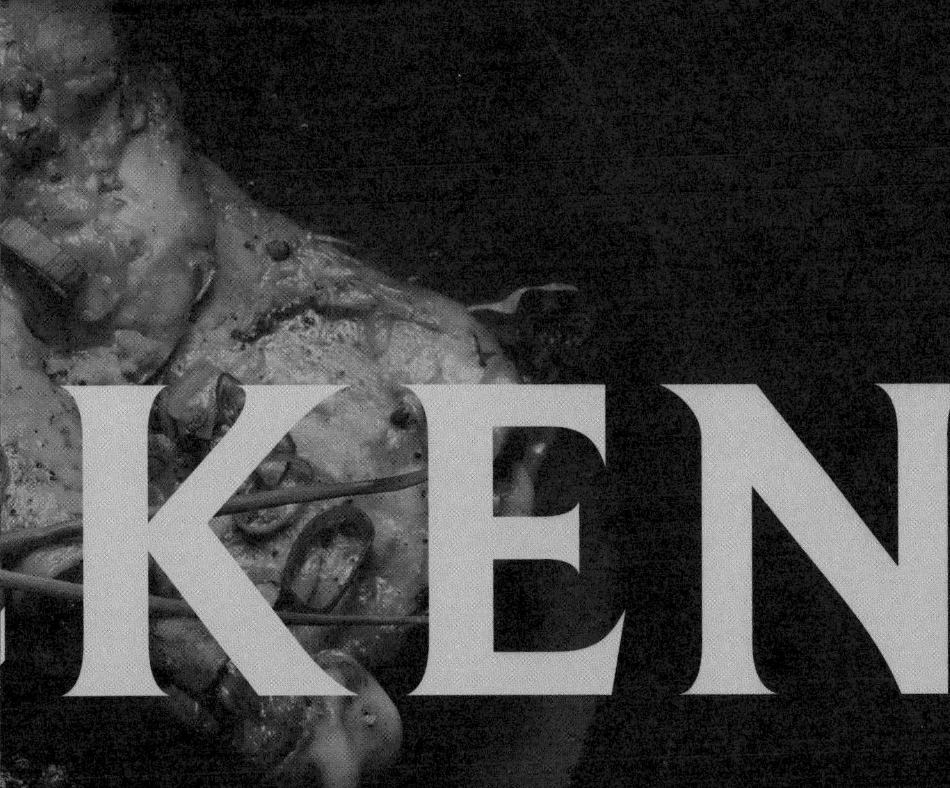
KEN

Spicy Peri-Peri Chicken Livers

Serves	Ingredients	Method
6–8	¼ cup olive oil	Heat 3 tbsp of the oil in a large frying pan over medium-high heat and fry the livers until browned, about 2 minutes on each side. Set aside to keep warm.

Ingredients

¼ cup olive oil
1 kg chicken livers
2 medium-sized onions, finely chopped
4 garlic cloves, crushed
3 medium-sized tomatoes, grated
½ cup tomato paste
1 tsp dried oregano
1 tsp peri-peri powder (see note page 83) or
   dried chilli flakes
2 tbsp chicken spice, or substitute with
   1 tbsp salt and ½ tbsp pepper
1 tbsp dried thyme
fresh red chilli and coriander leaves,
   finely chopped, to garnish (optional)
potato bread (see recipe page 156) or other
   bread of choice, to serve (optional)

Method

Heat 3 tbsp of the oil in a large frying pan over medium-high heat and fry the livers until browned, about 2 minutes on each side. Set aside to keep warm.

Heat the remaining oil in a separate frying pan and fry the onion and garlic until golden brown and soft, about 5 minutes.

Add the cooked chicken livers, tomatoes, tomato paste, oregano, peri-peri powder, chicken spice and thyme to the onion mixture, stir, and cook over a low heat until a thick, rich sauce has formed, about 25 minutes.

Season, garnish with chopped red chilli and coriander, if using, and serve with potato bread or other bread of choice on the side if desired.

"This was a firm favourite when the family were visiting Tata's house at Qunu in the Eastern Cape. When I would ask them what they would like for breakfast, all the children and the grandchildren wanted was these chicken livers, every single day. But only at Qunu, never back home in the city!"

Sweet Chutney Chicken

Serves

....

4–6

Ingredients

....

1 tbsp paprika

1 tsp white pepper

1 tbsp chicken spice, or substitute with
½ tbsp salt and ¼ tbsp pepper

1 whole chicken (approx. 1.25 kg)
cut into 8 pieces

1½ cups sweet fruit chutney

1 cup mayonnaise

4 tbsp medium-heat curry powder

2 cups water

charred lemon slices and spinach,
to serve (optional)

....

Image on previous page

Method

....

Preheat the oven to 180°C.

Put the paprika, pepper and chicken
spice in a small bowl, mix to combine,
and rub into the chicken pieces.

Arrange chicken pieces in an ovenproof
dish and cook for 15 minutes.

While the chicken is cooking, combine
the chutney, mayonnaise, curry powder
and water in a medium-sized bowl,
mixing well.

Cover the chicken with the chutney
mixture.

Lower the oven temperature to 160°C,
return the chicken to the oven, and cook
for a further 30 minutes, or until golden
brown and cooked through.

Serve sliced on a bed of spinach leaves,
with reserved sauce poured over.
Garnish with charred lemon slices,
if desired.

Thyme Roast Chicken with Sweet Potato

Serves	Ingredients	Method
6–8	1 chicken, cut into 8 pieces, skin removed	Preheat the oven to 180°C.

Ingredients

1 chicken, cut into 8 pieces, skin removed

1 tbsp paprika

1 tbsp chicken spice, or substitute with
  ½ tbsp salt and ¼ tbsp pepper

3 medium-sized sweet potatoes,
  cut into large chunks

1 tbsp chopped fresh thyme leaves

3 tbsp olive oil

1 large onion, chopped

microgreens to garnish (optional)

....

Image on following page

Method

Preheat the oven to 180°C.

Arrange the chicken pieces in a large roasting pan and season with paprika and chicken spice. Scatter over the sweet potato. Sprinkle with the thyme and salt and pepper. Drizzle with 2 tbsp of the oil and mix to coat.

Sauté onion in the remaining oil until golden brown, taking care not to burn. Remove the chicken and potatoes from the oven and mix together with the sautéed onion.

Serve scattered with microgreens, if using.

Coriander Chicken Curry

Serves	Ingredients	Method
6	2 garlic cloves	Blend the garlic and red chillies to a smooth paste in the blender.
	2 fresh red chillies, chopped	
	2 medium-sized tomatoes	Bring a small pot of water to the boil, add the tomatoes and cook until skin is burst, about 20 to 30 seconds. Once cool, grate tomatoes.
	200 ml vegetable oil	
	1 medium-sized onion, sliced	
	4 tbsp masala curry powder	
	2 tbsp grated fresh ginger	Pour the oil into a large, heavy casserole dish and place over medium heat. Sauté onion until golden brown. Add the masala curry powder, ginger, garlic and chilli paste, and turmeric. Add chicken and salt, mix well and cook for 10–15 minutes until fragrant.
	2 tsp turmeric powder	
	1 kg chicken, any combination of wings and drumsticks	
	1 tsp salt	
	½ cup curry leaves	
	1 handful fresh coriander, stalks removed	Add the curry leaves, three-quarters of the coriander and chicken stock and simmer for approximately 30 minutes, adding water if needed.
	1 cup chicken stock	
	microgreens, to serve (optional)	

Add tomatoes and remaining coriander, and continue to simmer on low heat until meat is tender.

Garnish with microgreens, if using, and serve.

Umleqwa with Umhluzi
Free-Range Farm Chicken with Gravy

Serves	Ingredients	Method
4–6	1 large farm chicken (approx. 1 kg), cut into 8 pieces 1 medium-sized onion, roughly chopped 3 cups water, plus 1 cup for the gravy 2 tbsp cake flour (see note page 52) spring onion, some chopped, to garnish (optional)	Place the chicken pieces, onion and 2 cups of water in a large pot and bring to the boil. Cook until the water has evaporated, about 1 hour and 30 minutes. The chicken will braise in its own fat until golden brown. Add remaining cup of water and cook until chicken is cooked through, about 30 minutes. Check, piercing a chicken breast with the tip of knife; the juices will run clear when it is cooked through. To make the gravy, whisk 1 cup of water with the flour to make a paste and add to the pot with the chicken. Continue cooking until a thick gravy forms, about 10 minutes. Season with salt and pepper, garnish with spring onion, if using, and serve.

"The first time I served this to Tata I didn't make umhluzi (gravy). He immediately called me over to the table and asked, 'Why is this chicken not drinking?' I rushed back to the kitchen and quickly made umhluzi – and made sure umleqwa was then always served with umhluzi!"

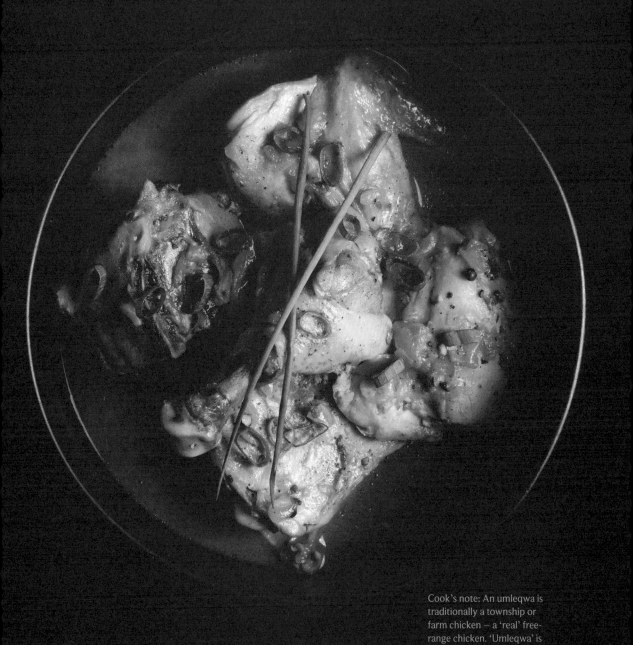

Cook's note: An umleqwa is traditionally a township or farm chicken — a 'real' free-range chicken. 'Umleqwa' is an isiXhosa word meaning 'a chicken that you have to chase'.

"I like relaxing at the house, reading quietly, taking in the sweet smell that comes from the pots, sitting around a table with the family."

— Nelson Mandela

ME

Mama Xoliswa's Meatballs

Serves	Ingredients	Method
6–8	600 g lean beef mince 2 medium-sized onions, grated 4 medium-sized tomatoes, grated 2 tbsp chopped fresh rosemary leaves $^2/_3$ cup cake flour (see note page 52) 2 large eggs, lightly beaten oil for frying 1 beef stock cube dissolved in ½ cup boiling water Parsley, finely chopped, to garnish (optional)	Put the mince, onion, tomato, rosemary and three-quarters of the flour in a medium-sized bowl. Season and mix well. Add the beaten eggs, mix to combine, and then shape into small ovals. Heat the oil in a pan over medium heat and fry the meatballs in batches for about 10 minutes, until browned on the outside and cooked through inside. Drain excess oil from the pan and set meatballs aside to keep warm. Mix the stock with the remaining flour, stirring until smooth, then pour into the pan. Turn heat to high, and stir continuously until a rich gravy is formed. Pour gravy over meatballs to serve, garnish with parsley, if desired.

Stuffed Roasted Rolled Beef

Serves	Ingredients	
8–10	2 kg rolled beef	1 tbsp grated fresh ginger
		2 garlic cloves, chopped
	Marinade	3 large carrots, chopped
	2 tbsp paprika	1 cup button mushrooms, chopped
	1 tbsp chopped fresh rosemary leaves	2 handfuls spinach, chopped
	1 tbsp dried oregano	1 cup celery leaves, chopped
	1 tbsp coarsely ground black pepper	1 tbsp cornflour
	1 garlic clove, thinly sliced	1 tbsp chopped fresh mint leaves
	2 cups cola	1 beef stock cube dissolved in 1 cup boiling water
	Stuffing	cauliflower purée (see recipe page 141), green herb oil (see recipe page 147) and steamed green beans, to serve
	¼ cup vegetable oil	microgreens, to garnish (optional)
	1 large onion, chopped	

Method

Cut the beef roll open so you have one big, flat piece.

To make the marinade, combine the paprika, rosemary, oregano, pepper, sliced garlic and cola in a large bowl, season, and mix well. Add the meat to the marinade mixture, turning to coat well, and leave to marinate for 1 hour.

To make the stuffing, heat the oil in a saucepan over medium heat. Add the onion and sauté until golden brown. Add the ginger, chopped garlic, carrots, mushrooms and spinach. Season and cook, stirring, until vegetables are cooked.

Combine the cornflour with a little water and add to the saucepan along with the mint and stock. Simmer until it achieves a gravy-like consistency, then set aside to cool slightly.

After 1 hour take the meat out of the marinade and lay it out on a flat surface. Arrange the stuffing on top of the meat. Using string, carefully roll the meat up, making sure the vegetables stay inside, and tie in as many places as needed to hold the roll together. Transfer to a baking dish and roast for 45 minutes each side, or until the meat is browned on the outside and juicy inside.

Slice the meat carefully, removing the string. Serve on a bed of freshly steamed green beans with cauliflower purée and green herb oil, and sauce from the roasting dish. Garnish with microgreens, if using.

....

Also see image on following page

Umsila Wenkomo
Slow-Roasted Oxtail

Serves

8–10

Ingredients

3 kg oxtail, excess fat removed

6 celery stalks, chopped

6 large carrots, chopped

1 large onion, chopped

3 garlic cloves, crushed

3 tbsp chopped fresh rosemary leaves

3 tbsp chopped fresh thyme leaves

2 tsp paprika

2 tbsp barbeque spice, or substitute
with 1 tbsp salt and ½ tbsp pepper

1 cup red wine

1 cup tomato paste

60g (1 packet) oxtail soup powder (available
from your supermarket or grocery store)

boiled baby potatoes and steamed baby
carrots and green beans, to serve

Method

Put the oxtail in a large pot over medium-high heat with enough water to cover. Bring to the boil, add the celery, carrots, onion and garlic together with the rosemary, thyme, paprika and barbeque spice and simmer for 30 minutes until vegetables are soft, then reduce the heat and cover. Braise for 1 hour with lid on until the meat is soft and starts to brown in its own fat. Add wine, tomato paste, and more water to cover.

Mix the packet of soup with a little water to make a paste, then add to the meat. Cook for a further 1 ½ hours with lid on, until the meat is soft but still on the bones, checking regularly to make sure that there is still enough liquid to cover.

Remove from the heat, separate the meat from the vegetables and sauce, and use a strainer to strain the vegetables out of the sauce to get a thick, smooth sauce. Discard the vegetables and add meat back to the sauce.

Serve with baby potatoes and steamed baby carrots and green beans.

"Whenever I cooked oxtail stew with samp and beans (see recipe page 64) Tata would call people to come and eat with him. Two of these people were Uncle Kathy (Ahmed Kathrada) and Tata Walter (Sisulu). They would come every Wednesday, because that's when we cooked oxtail, and Uncle Kathy always had to have his own parcel to take home."

Ginger Pork & Vegetable Stir Fry

Serves	Ingredients	Method

6–8

Marinade

2 tbsp vegetable oil

3 tbsp lemon juice

2 tbsp soy sauce

3 tbsp grated fresh ginger

1 tbsp paprika

1 tbsp chopped fresh thyme leaves
or dried thyme

1 vegetable stock cube, dissolved in
1 cup of boiling water

1 kg pork tenderloin, trimmed and
thinly sliced

2 red onions, sliced

2 baby marrows (zucchini), thinly sliced

1 cup snow peas (mangetout) or
sugar snap peas

1 red pepper (capsicum), seeds removed
and sliced lengthwise

microgreens, to garnish (optional)

Combine 1 tablespoon oil, lemon juice, soy sauce, ginger, paprika, thyme and stock in a medium-size bowl and mix well. Add pork, turn to coat well, and leave to marinate for 5–10 minutes.

Heat the remaining oil in a non-stick frying pan over medium heat. Add the onion, baby marrow and snow peas and pepper and cook for 5–10 minutes, stirring frequently, until tender but still crisp. Add the pork with marinade to the vegetables, and fry, stirring, until the sauce has reduced and become thick.

Season, garnish with microgreens, if desired, and serve.

Mushroom Pork Chops

Serves

8

Ingredients

Pork chops

8 x 100 g pork chops

1 tsp chicken spice, or substitute with
  ¼ tsp salt and ¹/₈ tsp pepper

2 tsp dried thyme

2 tbsp olive oil

fried mushrooms, thinly sliced red capsicums,
  microgreens and extra sauce, to serve
  (optional)

Mushroom sauce

2 medium-sized onions, sliced into
  thick rounds

2 garlic cloves, finely chopped

250 g white button mushrooms, thickly sliced

2 cups fresh cream

2 tbsp cake flour (see note page 52)

¼ cup water

Method

Preheat the oven to 180°C.

Rub the chops all over with the chicken spice, thyme and salt and white pepper.

Heat the oil in a large frying pan over medium-high heat and fry the chops until golden brown, about 5 minutes on each side.

Transfer the chops to an ovenproof dish and bake for 20 minutes.

While the chops are cooking, to make the mushroom sauce, fry the onion in the pan used for the chops until soft and golden, about 5 minutes. Add the garlic and mushrooms and cook for a further 2 minutes.

Add the cream and cook over a medium heat until reduced by about one-third.

To thicken the sauce, mix the flour and water to make a smooth paste and add to the mushroom mixture. Cook over a low heat, stirring continuously until smooth and thick, about 5 minutes. Season.

Add the chops to the sauce, cover and cook in the oven for 15 minutes.

Garnish with microgreens if desired, and serve with fried mushrooms, thinly sliced red capsicums and extra sauce.

Pork
Belly

Serves	Ingredients	Method
2–3	500 g pork belly	Preheat the oven to 160°C.

Serves: 2–3

Ingredients:
500 g pork belly
2 chicken stock cubes, dissolved in 2 cups boiling water
1 cup soy sauce
1 cup freshly squeezed orange juice
1 tbsp allspice
2 tbsp brown sugar
1 tbsp grated fresh ginger
2 tbsp vegetable oil
microgreens, to garnish (optional)
rice-stuffed peppers, to serve (see recipe page 142)

Method:

Preheat the oven to 160°C.

Place the pork belly in an ovenproof dish. Put the stock, soy sauce, orange juice, allspice, sugar, ginger and oil in a medium-sized bowl and stir to combine.

Pour the mixture over the pork belly and cover with foil.

Roast for about 2 hours. Remove foil and roast for a further 30 minutes, until tender but crispy on the edges. Slice into portions.

Garnish with microgreens, if desired, and serve with rice-stuffed peppers and sauce from the roasting dish.

Braised Lamb Shank

3—4

Ingredients

2 medium-sized tomatoes

2 tbsp vegetable oil

1 large onion, chopped

4 lamb shanks

1 tbsp barbeque spice, or substitute with
½ tbsp salt and ¼ tbsp pepper

1 tbsp paprika

2 tbsp chopped fresh rosemary leaves

1 cup white wine

3 cups chicken stock

2 tbsp tomato paste

2 celery sticks, chopped

2 carrots, roughly chopped

1 garlic clove, peeled

3 fresh rosemary sprigs

Method

Bring a small pot of water to the boil, add the tomatoes and cook until skin is burst, about 20 to 30 seconds. Once cool, chop tomatoes.

Heat the oil in a large casserole dish over low heat, and sauté the onion until golden brown.

Put the lamb shanks in a large bowl and season with the barbeque spice, paprika and rosemary. Add to the onion and braise until brown, about 15 minutes, turning throughout. Add wine and stock, bring to the boil and cook, covered, for 10 minutes. Add tomatoes, tomato paste, celery, carrots, garlic clove and rosemary sprigs and cook for 1 hour, or until the meat is tender, the vegetables are soft, and the sauce is thick and brown.

Serve with a potato side dish of your choice.

Spicy Lamb Knuckle Stew

Serves	Ingredients	Method
6–8	3 large tomatoes	Bring a small pot of water to the boil, add the tomatoes and cook until skin is burst, about 20 to 30 seconds. Once cool, chop tomatoes.
	2 tbsp olive oil	
	2 kg lamb knuckles	
	l large red onion, chopped	
	1 tsp paprika	Heat the oil in a large heavy-based, saucepan over medium-high heat. Add the lamb knuckles, onion, paprika, and turmeric, mix well, and braise until meat is browned, about 15 minutes.
	1 tbsp turmeric powder	
	2 tbsp fresh chopped red or green chillies, or 1 tbsp dried chilli flakes	
	2 tbsp honey	
	2 lamb stock cubes, dissolved in 2 cups of water	Add the tomatoes, cover and cook for a further 20 minutes.
	1 fresh fennel bulb, sliced	
	1 tbsp chopped fresh basil leaves	Reduce the heat to low and add chillies, honey, stock and fennel, and season. Cook until meat is soft and tender and the sauce has thickened, about 1 hour.
	boiled potatoes, to serve (or other vegetable of choice)	
	microgreens, to garnish (optional)	
		To keep the aroma and flavour fresh, add the basil 5 minutes before serving.
	Image on previous page	Serve with boiled potatoes or other vegetable of choice, garnished with microgreens, if using.

Lamb
Pot Roast

Serves	Ingredients	Method
6–8	1.5 kg leg of lamb, on the bone	Preheat the oven to 180°C.

Serves: 6–8

Ingredients:

1.5 kg leg of lamb, on the bone

3 garlic cloves, sliced lengthways

3 cups water

3 tbsp barbeque spice, or substitute with
   1 ½ tbsp salt and ¾ tbsp pepper

¼ cup lemon juice

1 tsp white pepper

1 tbsp cake flour (see note page 52)

vegetables of your choice, to serve

rosemary sprigs, freshly chopped chives,
   and thinly sliced red onion and red pepper
   (capsicum), to garnish (optional)

. . . .

Image on following page

Method:

Preheat the oven to 180°C.

Cut thin slits into the lamb with a sharp knife and insert the garlic slivers.

Combine the water, barbeque spice, lemon juice and pepper and pour into the bottom of a roasting pan. Place the lamb on top of the liquid and cover with foil.

Roast until the lamb is tender, about 1 hour. Remove the foil and continue roasting until the lamb is browned, about 15 minutes, checking the liquid level and adding a little water if it is in danger of drying out and sticking to the pan. Remove the meat from the pan and set aside to rest for 15 minutes before carving.

Mix the flour with a little water and add this to the meat juices at the bottom of the roasting pan. Stir over a medium heat on the stove until you have a thick gravy.

Slice the lamb and serve with the gravy and vegetables of your choice, garnished with rosemary sprigs, chives and thinly sliced red onion and pepper, if desired.

Soy Sauce Lamb Chops

Serves	Ingredients	Method

Serves

4–6

Ingredients

1 tbsp olive oil

1 tsp crushed garlic

½ tsp barbeque spice, or substitute with
   ¼ tsp salt and ⅛ tsp pepper

1 kg lamb loin chops

1 medium-sized onion, sliced into rings

1 cup tomato sauce or ketchup

½ cup soy sauce

1 tbsp dried oregano

onion rings (see recipe page 145) and
   vegetables of your choice, to serve

microgreens, to garnish (optional)

Method

Preheat the oven to 180°C.

Mix together the oil, garlic and barbeque spice. Rub the chops all over with the mixture.

Arrange the chops in a single layer in an ovenproof dish and bake for 20 minutes.

Gently fry the onions and mix together with the tomato sauce, soy sauce and oregano. Pour the mixture over the chops and return to the oven. Bake until the onions have caramelised and a thick, dark sauce has formed, about 15 minutes.

Serve hot with onion rings and vegetables of your choice, garnished with microgreens, if desired.

"A human being, whatever his colour may be . . . ought never to be compelled to regard taking meals as a mere duty."

— Nelson Mandela

SIDES,
& DRE

SAUCES
DRESSINGS

Umfino
Spinach with Red Peppers

Serves	Ingredients	Method
4–6 as a side	1 litre water	Put the water and stock cube into a saucepan and bring to the boil over medium-high heat. Add the spinach and cook for 5–8 minutes. Remove from the heat and strain off all the liquid.

Serves

4–6 as a side

Ingredients

1 litre water

1 vegetable stock cube

2 handfuls spinach, rinsed and chopped

4 tbsp olive oil

1 medium-sized onion, chopped

1 large red pepper (capsicum), deseeded and chopped

microgreens, to garnish (optional)

Method

Put the water and stock cube into a saucepan and bring to the boil over medium-high heat. Add the spinach and cook for 5–8 minutes. Remove from the heat and strain off all the liquid.

In another saucepan, heat the oil and fry the onion until soft and golden brown. Add red pepper and spinach, mix, and cook, stirring, for 5 minutes. Season with salt and pepper and simmer for a further 3–4 minutes.

Serve as a side, garnished with microgreens, if using.

....

Cook's note: Umfino, known as morogo in isiSotho, is a traditional dish made from wild spinach, cabbage and sometimes maize meal to make a vegetable pap. In this version, maize meal is omitted and store-bought or home-grown English spinach is complemented by the sweetness of red pepper.

Rosemary Baby Potatoes with Creamy Blue Cheese Sauce

Serves

4–6 as a side

Ingredients

1 kg baby potatoes

3 tbsp olive oil

2 tbsp chopped fresh rosemary leaves or dried rosemary, plus extra to serve

1 tsp salt

1 tsp pepper

creamy blue cheese sauce (see recipe page 148), to serve

Image on previous page

Method

Preheat the oven to 180°C.

Rinse the potatoes and dry with a paper towel.

Make evenly spaced cuts approximately ¼ to ½ cm apart into each potato, taking care not to slice all the way through.

Mix the oil, rosemary and salt and pepper in a large roasting pan, add potatoes and mix gently to coat.

Roast the potatoes for 20–40 minutes, turning occasionally, until golden.

Pour the blue cheese sauce over the hot potatoes, sprinkle with more rosemary, and serve.

"I love these potatoes so much I often make them for myself as a simple stand-alone dinner with a fresh garden salad – delicious!"

Xoli's Creamy Potatoes

Serves	Ingredients	Method

Serves

6–8 as a side

Ingredients

4 medium-sized potatoes, peeled
1 vegetable stock cube
125 ml vegetable oil
1 large onion, peeled and cut into thin rings
1 cup fresh cream
1 tbsp dried thyme
chopped spring onion, to garnish (optional)
flaky sea salt, for finishing

....

Image on following page

Method

Preheat the oven to 180°C.

Cut the potatoes into 1cm-thick rounds. Cook in boiling water with vegetable stock until tender but firm, about 10 minutes. Drain and set aside to cool.

Heat the oil in a frying pan over medium-high heat and fry the onions until soft and golden, about 5 minutes. Remove the onions from the oil with a slotted spoon and set aside. Fry the potatoes in the same pan, flipping them as they cook, for approximately 3 minutes each side or until golden.

Alternate layers of potato and onion in one large ovenproof dish or smaller, individual dishes.

Season with salt and pepper. Pour cream over and sprinkle with thyme.

Bake until the potatoes are cooked through and the top is golden brown, about 30 minutes.

Serve hot, sprinkled with chopped spring onion, if using, and flaky sea salt.

Roast Mixed Vegetables
with Kale & Feta

Serves

4–6 as a side

Ingredients

1 cup sliced sweet potatoes

1 cup sliced carrots

1 large red onion, chopped

1 large butternut squash (see note page 54), peeled and cut into cubes

1 cup broccoli florets

1 tbsp chopped fresh rosemary leaves

2 tbsp vegetable oil

2 cups shredded kale

1 cup crumbled feta

Method

Preheat the oven to 160°C.

Put the sweet potatoes, carrots, onion, butternut, broccoli, rosemary and oil in an ovenproof dish. Season with salt and pepper and roast for 30 minutes or until the vegetables are crunchy.

Sprinkle with the kale and feta, then roast for a further 5 minutes.

Cauliflower Purée with Green Herb Oil

Approx. 1 cup

1 cup chopped cauliflower
¼ cup melted butter
1 tbsp olive oil
1 small onion, chopped
2 cloves garlic, chopped
500 ml fresh cream
green herb oil (see recipe page 147), to serve

....

See image on pages 108–9

Preheat the oven to 180°C.

Arrange the cauliflower in an ovenproof dish or tray and season with salt and pepper. Pour over the melted butter, tossing to coat. Roast cauliflower until golden brown.

Heat the oil in a large frying pan over medium-high heat and fry onion and garlic until soft. Add the roasted cauliflower and cream and let it simmer until the cream has reduced into a thick sauce. Season with salt and pepper and blend the mixture with a blender until soft and creamy.

Drizzle the green herb oil over the cauliflower purée and serve.

Rice-Stuffed Peppers

Makes	Ingredients	Method

3

Ingredients

4 tbsp olive oil

1 medium-sized onion, chopped

1 tsp crushed garlic

1 red pepper (capsicum), deseeded and chopped

1 cup shredded kale

2 medium-sized carrots, grated

1 cup basmati or long-grain cooked rice

3 large red peppers (capsicum)

Method

Heat the oil in a saucepan over medium heat and sauté the onion. Add the garlic, chopped pepper, kale and carrots and stir to combine well.

Lower the heat and keep stirring until vegetables are softened. Add the rice and mix well. Remove from the heat.

Preheat the oven to 180°C.

Halve or cut the tops off the peppers and remove the seeds. Place the peppers in an ovenproof dish and stuff them with the rice mixture.

Roast for 20–30 minutes.

Tomato & Red Onion Salsa in a Poppadom Basket

Makes	Ingredients	Method
6	oil for deep frying	Heat the oil in the deep fryer.
	6 store-bought poppadoms	
	3 large ripe tomatoes	Drop the poppadoms, one at a time, into the deep fryer. Using two stainless-steel soup spoons, hold each poppadom with one spoon and press the middle to form a round basket shape with the other. This needs be done very fast as the poppadom only takes a few seconds to cook.
	1 large red onion, finely chopped	
	2 tbsp red wine vinegar	
	See image on page 79	
		Remove from the oil and drain carefully on a paper towel.
		Bring a small pot of water to the boil, add the tomatoes and cook until skin is burst, about 20 to 30 seconds. Once cool, deseed and chop tomatoes.
		Mix together the tomatoes, onion and vinegar in a bowl. Season with salt and serve in the poppadom baskets.

Onion Rings

Makes
Approx. 8–10 rings

Ingredients

1 cup vegetable oil

1 medium-sized onion, sliced into rings

2 eggs, beaten

1 cup cake flour (see note page 52), seasoned with salt and pepper

....

See image on page 127

Method

Pour the oil into a frying pan over medium-high heat.

While it heats, coat the onion rings. First dip the onion rings into the beaten egg, then into the seasoned flour, making sure they are well coated.

Fry the onion rings for 2–3 minutes or until golden brown.

Citrus Dressing

Makes	Ingredients	Method
½ cup	2 tbsp lemon juice 2 tbsp orange juice 1 tbsp olive oil 1 tbsp wine vinegar	Blend or whisk all ingredients together with salt and pepper to season until emulsified and thick.

Coriander & Lime Dressing

Makes	Ingredients	Method
½ cup	100 g fresh coriander, including stalks, chopped 1 garlic clove, chopped 1 tbsp lime juice 2 tbsp honey 1 tsp salt 250 ml olive oil	Blend all of the ingredients together until combined.

Cider Vinaigrette

Makes	Ingredients	Method
½ cup	3 tbsp olive oil 3 tbsp cider vinegar 1 tsp salt 1 tsp coarsely ground white pepper	Whisk all ingredients together in a small bowl until combined.

Green Herb Oil

Makes	Ingredients	Method
2 cups	3 tbsp chopped fresh parsley 3 tbsp chopped fresh coriander leaves 3 tbsp chopped fresh celery leaves 3 tbsp chopped fresh thyme leaves 2 cups olive oil .... Cook's note: You can also use this as a delicious fresh salad dressing or as a garnish for meat dishes.	Place the herbs and oil in a saucepan. Simmer gently on low heat until the oil is green in colour. Let it cool and strain with a clean cloth. Will keep in the fridge indefinitely. .... See image on pages 108–9

Creamy Cheese Sauce

Makes	Ingredients	Method
1 cup	2 tbsp vegetable oil 1 large onion, chopped 2 garlic cloves, chopped 500 ml fresh cream 1 cup Parmesan, grated .... See image on page 76	Heat the oil in a saucepan over medium heat and sauté the onion and garlic until golden brown. Add the cream, stirring, and then the Parmesan. Stir for 5 minutes until the sauce is thick and creamy. Strain the sauce before serving to make it extra smooth.

Creamy Blue Cheese Sauce

Makes	Ingredients	Method
1 cup	1 tbsp butter 500 ml fresh cream 1 cup blue cheese, cut or crumbled into small pieces 1 tbsp chopped fresh rosemary leaves .... See image on page 135	Melt the butter in a saucepan over medium heat. Add the cream and the cheese and stir for 5 minutes or until the cheese has melted and a creamy sauce has formed. Stir in the rosemary and serve.

Mushroom Sauce

Makes

1 ½ cups

Ingredients

2 tbsp olive oil

2 medium-sized onions,
  sliced into thick rounds

2 garlic cloves, finely chopped

250 g white button mushrooms, thickly sliced

2 cups fresh cream

2 tbsp cake flour (see note page 52)

¼ cup water

Method

Heat the oil in a frying pan over medium-high heat. Fry the onion until soft and golden, about 5 minutes. Add the garlic and mushrooms and cook for 2 minutes.

Add the cream and cook over a medium heat until reduced by one-third.

Mix the flour and water to make a smooth paste and add to the mushroom mixture. Cook over a low heat, stirring continuously until smooth, about 5 minutes. Season.

BRE

AD

Delicious Dombolo Dumplings

Makes	Ingredients	
8–10	5 cups cake flour (see note page 52)	10 g (1 sachet) instant dry yeast
	1 tsp salt	2½ cups lukewarm water
	1 tsp brown sugar	2 tbsp butter

Method

Sift the flour and salt into a large bowl and mix in the sugar and yeast. Gradually add the water, mixing until a soft dough is formed (the amount will vary according to the humidity in the air).

Knead the dough in the bowl until smooth and elastic, then cover the bowl with plastic wrap and set aside in a warm place until doubled in size, about 1 hour.

Take lumps of dough and roll them into balls the size of your palm.

Boil a kettle full of water.

Put the butter into a large, heavy, lidded pot over medium heat and leave to melt.

Place the balls of dough in the melted butter and pour boiling water into the pot to a depth of 2 cm.

Cover (leaving a small gap for some of the steam to escape) and cook for 20 minutes. As the water evaporates, the butter will begin to fry the base of the dumplings; keep an eye on them to make sure they don't catch and burn and add a little more water if needed.

Serve hot.

Cook's note: Dombolo is a
traditional type of steamed bread,
often served as a side with stews.

Umbhako
Pot Bread

Ingredients
....

butter or margarine, for greasing
6 cups bread flour
1½ tsp salt
2 tsp brown sugar

10 g (1 sachet) instant dry yeast
lukewarm water as needed
oil, for greasing

Method

Use a large, heavy, lidded pot. Grease both the lid and the pot with the butter or margarine.

Sift the flour and salt into a large bowl. Add the salt, sugar and yeast and mix to combine.

Slowly incorporate enough lukewarm water to form a stiff dough (the amount will vary according to the humidity in the air). Tip onto a lightly floured surface and knead until firm but elastic.

Transfer the dough to a lightly oiled bowl, cover with a clean, damp cloth or cling wrap and set aside in a warm place until doubled in a size, 30–40 minutes.

Knock down the dough in the bowl and knead again, then roll into a ball and place in the greased pot. Put the lid on and set aside until the dough has once more doubled the size – almost to the top of the pot.

Put the pot on the stove over a low heat and cook, covered, until the crust has set, about 30 minutes.

Tip the bread out of the pot, turn it over, and return to the pot. Cover and cook for a further 30 minutes, until it has a golden-brown crust.

Tip the bread out of the pot and let it cool slightly before serving.

Store the bread wrapped in a clean cloth to keep it soft.

"Also known as potbrood,
traditionally this bread was made
on an open fire, but for this recipe
all you need is a sturdy pot for
your stovetop."

Potato Bread

Makes	Ingredients	Method
1 loaf	1 cup vegetable oil 4 large potatoes, peeled and grated 1 large onion, grated 2 large eggs, beaten 85 g cake flour (see note page 52) 2 tsp baking powder 1 tsp dried oregano 1 tsp dried thyme	Preheat the oven to 180°C. Put the oil in an oven tray and place in oven to heat. Place the potato and onion in a large bowl and mix to combine well. Stir in the eggs, cake flour, baking powder, oregano and thyme, season with salt and pepper and mix well. Transfer the potato mixture into the hot oil in the tray and bake until cooked through and golden brown on the outside, about 40 minutes. It will rise like regular bread and have a muffin-like texture. Allow to cool a little before slicing. Season and serve.

"This is a traditional Jewish dish
I learned to cook when I first came
to Johannesburg, which is served on
Friday's after shul (synagogue), and
is often accompanied by pâté."

TATA'S F
DESS

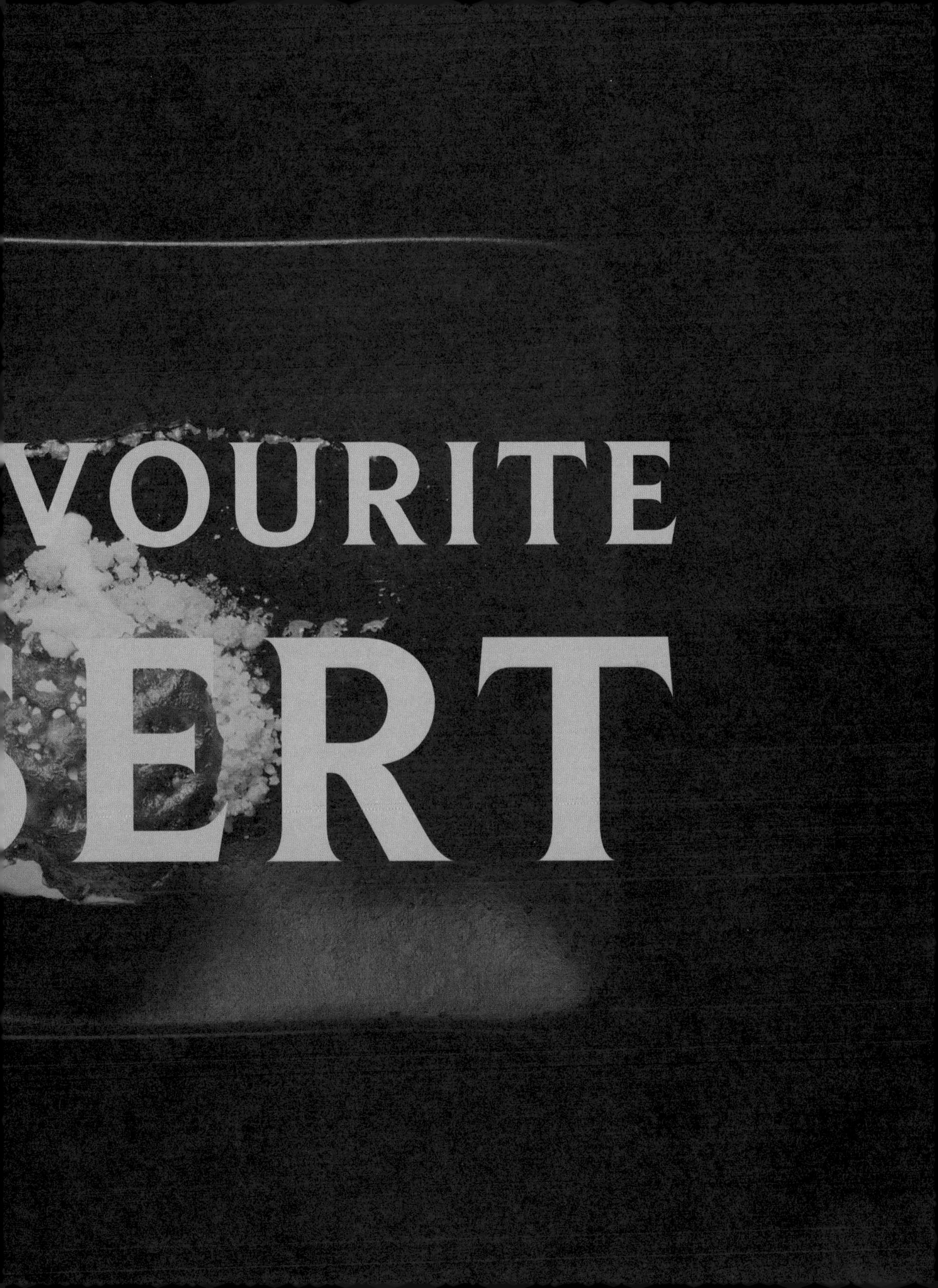
VOURITE
ERT

Malva
Pudding

Ingredients

Pudding

2 cups cake flour (see note page 52)

2 tbsp baking soda

1 cup brown sugar

4 eggs

4 tbsp butter or margarine, melted

2 cups milk

2 tbsp white vinegar

2 tbsp apricot jam

Caramel sauce

125 ml melted butter

125 g caster sugar

225 ml cream or milk

Berry compote

½ cup mixed frozen berries

2 tbsp lemon zest

1 tbsp honey

Amarula custard

70 ml water

125 ml melted butter

185 g white sugar

120 ml cream

1 tsp vanilla essence

60 ml Amarula Cream

To serve (optional)

ginger snap

biscuit crumbs

Cook's note: Amarula Cream is a South African creamy liqueur made from the fruit of the marula tree which is indigenous to southern Africa. It imparts a distinctly nutty flavour to the custard and is worth trying to source but if you can't get it, brandy or fortified sweet wine will suffice in its place.

Method overleaf

Tata's Favourite Dessert

Method

Preheat the oven to 190°C.

To make the pudding, mix the flour, baking soda and a pinch of salt together in a large bowl.

Put the sugar and eggs into another bowl and beat until smooth and creamy. Mix in butter, milk, vinegar and apricot jam. Add wet mixture to dry ingredients and combine.

Pour the mixture into a deep non-stick muffin tray, or brioche or dariole moulds. Bake for 30–35 minutes.

To make the caramel sauce, combine all ingredients in a saucepan over medium heat. Bring to the boil and cook for 5–10 minutes, until reduced and a syrupy sauce is formed.

To make the berry compote, place mixed frozen berries, lemon zest and honey in saucepan over medium heat. Bring to the boil. Lower heat and simmer until combined and a thick sauce forms, stirring frequently.

To make the custard, put water, butter and sugar in a saucepan over medium heat and bring to the boil. Turn down the heat and simmer for 2 minutes, stirring all the time. Stir in the cream, vanilla essence and Amarula Cream and remove from the heat.

To assemble, first garnish the plates with the berry compote.

Place a hot pudding on top of the compote.

Prick the pudding with a toothpick and pour over the caramel sauce so it soaks into the pudding.

Pour the Amarula custard over the pudding and serve, with ginger snap and biscuit crumbs on the side, if using.

Tata's Favourite Dessert

"There is some mystery about how this much-loved traditional pudding got its name. Some think it refers to Malvasia, a fortified sweet wine, while others say it could be derived from the malva plant that was used in South Africa's Cape region as a substitute for rose water. Yet others speculate it is derived from the Afrikaans term *malva lekker*, meaning 'marshmallow' in reference to its light, spongy texture. Regardless of how it was named, whilst Tata generally didn't indulge in sugar or sweets, he always ate my malva pudding!"

Conversion Tables

Abbreviations

g	gram
kg	kilogram
oz	ounce
lb	pound
mm	millimetre
cm	centimetre
in	inch
ml	millilitre
fl oz	fluid ounce
tsp	teaspoon
dsp	dessertspoon
tbsp	tablespoon
°C	degrees Celsius
°F	degrees Fahrenheit

Cup & spoon conversions

The metric cup (1 cup = 250 ml) is used in most countries outside the United States.

spoon/cup	metric	US metric
½ tsp	2½ ml	2½ ml
1 tsp	5 ml	5 ml
1 dsp	10 ml	–
1 tbsp	15 ml	15 ml
1 tbsp (Australia)	20 ml	–
⅛ cup	30 ml	30 ml
¼ cup	65 ml	60 ml
⅓ cup	85 ml	80 ml
½ cup	125 ml	120 ml
⅔ cup	170 ml	160 ml
¾ cup	190 ml	180 ml
1 cup	250 ml	240 ml
1½ cups	375 ml	360 ml
2 cups	500 ml	480 ml
4 cups	1 litre	960 ml

Egg sizes

Each country has different minimal legal weights; the following weights are approximated for the purposes of conversion.

	Australia	*NZ*	*South Africa*	*UK*	*US*
around 35 g	—	Pullet (4)	Small	—	Peewee
around 43 g	Medium	Small (5)	Medium	Small	Small
around 53 g	Large	Standard (6)	Large	Medium	Medium
around 60 g	Extra Large	Large (7)	Very Large	Large	Large
around 70 g	Jumbo	Jumbo (8)	Jumbo	Very Large	Extra Large
around 75 g	King Size	—	Super Jumbo	—	Jumbo

Cream equivalents

Fat contents differ widely, but approximate conversions are as below. New Zealand only has one main type of cream, so you may need to adjust recipes that call for double cream by for example, simmering a cream sauce for longer. Both single and double cream are now widely available in most countries.

Australia	*NZ*	*South Africa*	*UK*	*US*
Light	Lite	Pouring	Single	Light
Single	Cream	Pouring	Single	Light
Thickened	Thickened	Whipping	Whipping	Light Whipping
Double	Cream	Double Thick	Double	Heavy

Weight conversions

metric	*imperial/US*
15 g	½ oz
30 g	1 oz (= 28 g, more precisely)
60 g	2 oz
90 g	3 oz
100 g	3½ oz
125 g	4½ oz
150 g	5 oz
175 g	6 oz
200 g	7 oz
225 g	8 oz
250 g	9 oz
300 g	10½ oz
325 g	11½ oz
350 g	12½ oz
375 g	13 oz
400 g	14 oz
450 g	16 oz (1 lb)
500 g	18 oz
1 kg	36 oz (2¼ lb)

Liquid conversions

metric	*imperial/US*
5 ml	⅙ fl oz
15 ml	½ fl oz
30 ml	1 fl oz (= 28 ml, more precisely)
60 ml	2 fl oz
90 ml	3 fl oz
100 ml	3½ fl oz
125 ml	4 fl oz (¼ pint US)
150 ml	5 fl oz (¼ pint imperial)
175 ml	6 fl oz
200 ml	7 fl oz
225 ml	8 fl oz (½ pint US)
250 ml	9 fl oz
280 ml	10 fl oz (½ pint imperial)
340 ml	12 fl oz (¾ pint US)
420 ml	15 fl oz (¾ pint imperial)
450 ml	16 fl oz (1 pint US)
500 ml	18 fl oz
560 ml	20 fl oz (1 pint imperial)
1 litre	36 fl oz (1¾ pints imperial, 2¼ pints US)

Length conversions

metric	imperial/US
½ cm (5 mm)	¼ in
1 cm	½ in
2.5 cm	1 in
5 cm	2 in
7½ cm	3 in
10 cm	4 in
12½ cm	5 in
15 cm	6 in
18 cm	7 in
20 cm	8 in
23 cm	9 in
25½ cm	10 in
28 cm	11 in
30 cm	12 in (1 foot)
40 cm	16 in

Oven temperatures

	Celsius	Fahrenheit	Gas
very cool	110°C	225°F	¼
	120°C	250°F	½
cool	140°C	275°F	1
	150°C	300°F	2
moderate	170°C	325°F	3
	180°C	350°F	4
moderate–hot	190°C	375°F	5
	200°C	400°F	6
hot	220°C	425°F	7
	230°C	450°F	8
very hot	240°C	475°F	9
	260°C	500°F	10

"This house was not just a house; it was a welcoming home. This hotel means a lot to me because it is still welcoming people to come and reflect on who Tata was and what he has given to people."

– Xoliswa Ndoyiya

SANCTUARY MANDELA

Sanctuary Mandela celebrates the life of iconic freedom fighter, peacemaker, statesman, and father of the South African nation, Nelson Rolihlahla Mandela (1918–2013), known to the world as Madiba, or simply Tata.

Sanctuary Mandela is built on the site of Nelson Mandela's former Houghton residence, and features elements from the original home. Madiba and members of his family lived at the Houghton residence between 1991 and 1998 (after which it became the headquarters of the Nelson Mandela Foundation until 2002). He was based here while negotiating the multi-party talks that led to South Africa's democratic rebirth, South Africa's famous 1995 Rugby World Cup win, the first democratic elections, and his presidency.

Images clockwise from top: The Presidential Suite at Sanctuary Mandela; Hotel staff member Reitumetse Riet; Lobby sitting room; Bathroom in the Presidential Suite; An image of Nelson Mandela boxing training adorns the hotel corridor; The Presidential Suite; Hotel staff member Mpumi Khanyile; The exterior and gardens of Sanctuary Mandela.

Paying homage to Madiba's depth of character and contemplative spirit, the hotel has been designed to achieve a blend of being a functional boutique hotel, while still reflecting its status as an iconic part of South African history through design elements, photographs personal to the house, and artworks and artifacts from the Nelson Mandela Foundation's archive.

Images clockwise from top left: The swimming pool at Sanctuary Mandela; Hotel staff member Sibusiso Qubeka; View across the top floor of the hotel; Hotel staff member Sally-Anne Grinter; The Presidential Suite at Sanctuary Mandela; A bronze sculpture of Nelson Mandela welcomes visitors to the hotel; Ceiling detail; Wine racks in the hotel's bar; Desk in the Presidential Suite; Hotel staff member Khanyo Kula.

The former president's home is owned
by the Nelson Mandela Foundation, a non-
profit organisation which focuses its work on
contributing to the making of just societies
by mobilising the legacy of Nelson Mandela,
providing public access to information on
his life and times, and convening dialogue
on critical social issues. Its key objective is
finding sustainable solutions to the problems
confronting humanity. It aims to become
a respected change agent in South Africa
and beyond, with a global audience and an
embedded practice of deep dialogue informed
by robust research, analysis and evaluation.

Right: Nelson Mandela peruses the morning paper in the entranceway of his Houghton residence circa 1994,
now the entrance to Sanctuary Mandela.

"Xoli, thank you for feeding us so well all these years."

— Madiba

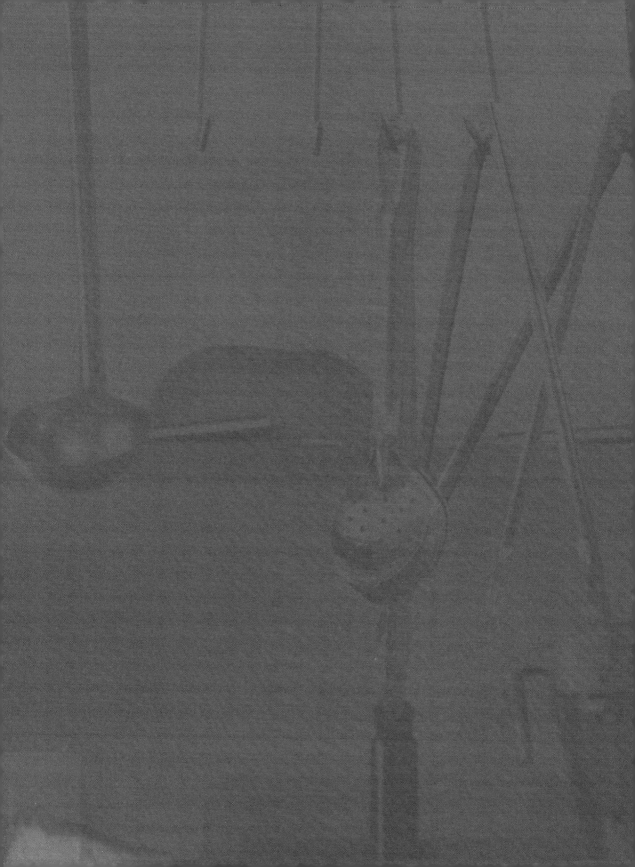

Index

Index

DF = Dairy Free   GF = Gluten Free   V = Vegetarian

Recipe names are denoted in bold; main ingredients are denoted in grey with corresponding recipes listed underneath. Page numbers denoted in italics indicate a photo. Note: Parmesan contains rennet and is not considered strictly vegetarian. Where it is listed as an ingredient, the recipe is denoted vegetarian on the basis that it can be substituted for a vegetarian Parmesan if desired. Most soy sauces contain gluten and where it is listed as an ingredient the recipe is denoted gluten free on the basis that those who have a gluten intolerance can substitute for a gluten-free soy sauce.

Acknowledgements

First and foremost I want to thank Tata Madiba for the opportunity he gave me, and for his daily words of wisdom. One of my favourites I will always remember is: "Remember not to give up in life, always remember who you are, and humble yourself." Thank you Tata, serving you was a great journey.

To my entire family, thank you for your love and understanding always: thank you to my mother for being a pillar of my strength and a hero to my children and my three beautiful grandchildren; to my children Mkhululi, Sinethemba, Mnqophiso and Lubambo, thank you for making it easy for me to serve Tata, for understanding my absence in your lives and for appreciating me as a mother that could still take care of you; to Pakama Mjobo, thank you for being a second mother to my children in good times and bad; to my brothers Madoda Ndembe and Madoda Ndoyiya for being father figures to my children and for giving them all the love that caring uncles could give, I'm eternally grateful; to my nieces and nephews, thank you for telling me how much you love me and for being the reason that I keep going, and to my niece Simthandile — thank you baby girl for your help with typing recipes day and night — you were *mafungwashe* for real! I love you all.

I would also like to thank: Gloria Nocanda for being a sister and a friend, and for believing in me and my cooking; Anna Trapido for seeing the potential to make my first book with me and for believing that I deserved to have one — thank you for being my caterpillar and turning into the butterflies of the future; the Mandela and Machel families for being my brothers and sisters and for allowing me the privilege of being a mother to your children, and a special thank you to Nandi Mandela for her warm and thoughtful foreword; Advocate Thando Tsetsewa for sharing your warm heart with me and forever making your home mine — you taught me the true definition of *ubuntu*; the Presidential Protection Unit for being our family when we were serving Tata, respecting and cherishing each other every day of our lives, and for keeping in touch now that Tata has left us; the medical team that took care of Tata and who worked with loyalty and dignity to serve him; my colleagues that served Tata and his family and were always respectful of my food whenever you served it; and last but not least to UDM leader Bantu Holomisa who was very important to Tata, thank you very much for being a big brother to us, joining Tata for meals at Qunu at any time of the day, driving all the way from Qunu to Queenstown to arrange telecoms in our homes so we could communicate with our families while we were at Qunu, you never complained but did it with love — and for home-baked bread and jam! Thank you.

To the team at the Nelson Mandela Foundation: Sello Hatang for making this book possible. From the first day I asked you for your help to make a second book you said, "Yes, Sis' Xoli, I will help you" and you really did; and Mandlenkosi Dakada, Verne Harris, Zandile Myeka, Zanele Riba, Razia Saleh and Buyi Sishuba for all their help — thank you.

Thanks to all the staff at Sanctuary Mandela for being another family for this second journey, and in particular the amazing kitchen team pictured opposite who prepared all the recipes featured in these pages, I thank you from the bottom of my heart; Dimitri Maritz for your wise words of encouragement to get on and do this book and leave the past in the past; and Vincent Monyake, Sally-Anne Grinter, Mpumi Khanyile, Khanyo Kula, Sibusiso Qubeka, Reitumetse Riet and everyone at the hotel for their gracious and invaluable assistance with the making of this book.

Lastly to Cameron Gibb for his beautiful photography and for making my dishes shine, and Ruth Hobday, Geoff Blackwell, Olivia van Velthooven, Nikki Addison, Sahm Venter and everyone at Blackwell & Ruth who helped with the making of this book, I thank you.

Top left to right — Nthabiseng Ramachela, Lesedi Kganyago, Tshiamo Maine, Mbali Ngcobo, Xoliswa Ndoyiya, Faith Jongman, Mordecai Brauns and Tendani Mahole; Bottom left to right — Thabang Qakisa, Xoliswa Ndoyiya, Unathi Jacobs and Nonsikelelo Fakude.

Produced and originated by Blackwell and Ruth Limited
PO Box 37692, Parnell, Auckland 1151, New Zealand
www.blackwellandruth.com

Publisher: Geoff Blackwell
Editor in Chief and Project Editor: Ruth Hobday
Design Director: Cameron Gibb
Layout: Olivia van Velthooven
Additional editorial: Nikki Addison and Tessa King

www.sanctuarymandela.com
www.nelsonmandelafoundation.org

ISBN: 978-0-473-67462-5

10 9 8 7 6 5 4 3 2 1

Manufactured in China by 1010 Printing Ltd.

This book is made with FSC®-certified paper and other controlled material and is printed with soy vegetable
inks. The Forest Stewardship Council® (FSC®) is a global, not-for-profit organisation dedicated to the
promotion of responsible forest management worldwide to meet the social, ecological, and economic rights
and needs of the present generation without compromising those of future generations.

Xoliswa ("Xoli") Ndoyiya was Nelson Mandela's personal chef for over 22 years until his death in 2013 at the age of 95. Born in the Eastern Cape and a native isiXhosa speaker, as was Madiba (Nelson Mandela's clan name), Xoli first moved to Johannesburg as a teenager.

In 1992 she started working for Nelson Mandela at the behest of a friend, at first cooking for Mandela, and then for his grandchildren and many friends that would frequently visit the house, as well as various national and international dignitaries and celebrities.

Today Ndoyiya is Chef de Tournant at the recently opened boutique luxury hotel Sanctuary Mandela, which is built on the site of Mandela's former Houghton residence where he lived from 1992 to 1998. She lives between Johannesburg and Komani (formerly Queenstown) in South Africa's Eastern Cape. *Made With Love* is her second book of recipes.